Beginners Guide To
Magic Crystals

Brittany Nightshade

Table of Contents

4

Forward

Hello and merry meet! My name is Brittany Nightshade and I've spent many years studying pagan traditions and writing books about all things relating to the metaphysical. It's long been a request of my readers to write a handbook that can be used for the purposes of reference regarding crystals as I frequently mention and use them in my own practice and writings.

This book contains an overview of many of the crystals and stones used in pagan practices, my goal is to make a quick reference guide in alphabetical order so that any time you need info about a specific stone you'll have it right at your fingertips in a compact easy to navigate book. I've noticed when visiting pagan shops that sell gems that there's usually a single page of information on the crystals they're selling which isn't helpful if you're new to the world of metaphysics and need a little more to go on. There are several books out there that aim to describe the properties and characteristics of gemstones but in my experience most of them are full of unnecessary filler that make them inconvenient for quick reference. I hope to remedy that and give you quick and concise information that you can rely on anytime and anywhere in a compact, concise book that you can carry with you when shopping for crystals or working on constructing your own magical rituals and meditations.

I wish you the best of luck in all your magical endeavors!
—Brittany Nightshade

Introduction

Rare stones and crystals have been found in nearly every archaeological study of ancient cultures, unfortunately many of the oldest civilizations lacked a way to record their history due to a lack of medium or lack of written language as most information was handed down verbally. However, research into these ancient civilizations has led us to the understanding that these lost cultures lived in tandem with the earth and the cycles of the celestial bodies and seasons so it would go to reason that the stones found on these sites, adorned to their clothing, placed in burial locations, and affixed to what would seem to be ritual tools, would play a huge part in their religious and spiritual practice.

As people search for meaning and purpose in this increasingly commodified society we live in, many are looking back to our ancestors for guidance on how to live a more fulfilled and spiritual life. As we become more and more alienated from our labor in the consumerist rat-race a part of our soul longs for the connection to the Earth that we once had, a connection that I believe is vital. With the advent of the internet, more and more people are gaining access to a near unlimited source of information, barriers of entry to earth based spiritual practices are constantly lowering as the gatekeeping esotericism of the 1900's fades for a more inclusionary mindset.

"But what about science?" one might ask. "Is there any actual evidence that these rocks do anything more than look pretty on a shelf or altar?" And the simple answer is "Yes." Everything on earth has a vibration and a charge, every atom in the universe vibrates at a specific frequency that is generally determined by the makeup of the object. This means that every crystal and every stone has its own vibrational frequency and those frequencies are released in the form of waves that can be detected by scientific instruments. There's a good chance that you make use of these properties in your day-to-day life and you might not even know it. Crystals are used in many consumer goods for their acoustic resonance properties; clocks, watches, radios, computers, cellphones, all these devices rely on the power of vibrating crystals and their unique properties to function properly.

While we know that ancient civilizations like the Sumerians, Egyptians, Native Americans, and Chinese used crystals and adorned their tools and garments with them we don't know the exact way in which these stones played a role in their day to day lives. We have some writings from ancient historians such as Pliny The Elder but those writings are few and far between and don't go into great detail outside of their practical usage. Modern practice takes inspiration from the information we do have about these cultures and combines them with more modern practices and is heavily influenced by eastern traditions, such as chakra work, which has also been practiced for thousands of years.

While there's no right or wrong way to use crystals, they do have measurable properties and are likely to be more effective if used in a way that considers those physical properties. Generally ritual tools are there to help you focus and direct your energies/intentions, but crystals are a power source of their own. For example, we often use a wand or athame for the purposes of directing our own energies, we light a candle to represent the element of fire and air to steel our focus for successful manifestation and the usage of those tools are typically very personal and vary from practitioner to practitioner. Crystals having inherent properties means that, for example, a black tourmaline crystal will always work to repel negative energies around us and a quartz crystal will always work to exercise negative energy and amplify our focus. Of course, any of these stones can be used in a variety of ways but their inherent properties should guide you in how you choose to apply them.

One could wax philosophical on the topic of crystals for ages, and people have for thousands of years, but that's not the aim of this book. One could get wrapped up in the science and history and inadvertently miss the point, crystals and precious stones are something that with a bit of base knowledge you can start your journey, you will learn more from using them in your day-to-day life than you ever will from any "authoritative" source. Spend some time learning the basics and work the ones that appeal to you into your practice in a way that works for you!

Aegirine

Integrity, Conviction, Morals

Aegirine is a stone of resilience. When under attack from the daily onslaught of negative energy brought on from work, social interactions, and any other day to day struggle. Aegirine helps you maintain your "self" amidst a barrage of negativity, as in the things you hold dear, your principles and convictions. It can be easy to react in a way that betrays our beliefs, anger and sadness are natural reactions to hostility and those emotional states might lead us to acting in a way we might regret when we're in a better headspace.

Carry Aegirine with you when you're expecting an especially difficult day or if you're going somewhere new, such as hiking on a new trail or visiting a new place. Any situation where you need to be at the top of your game and react in a rational, non-emotional way.

Aegirine activates the Root Chakra that is located at the base of the spine that dictates our physical ability to move and take action. When the Root Chakra isn't functioning properly it can lead to low levels of physical energy leaving you feeling tired and lacking motivation. Meditate with aegirine and focus on your energy stores being replenished while visualizing the vitality returning to your body.

Agate

Confidence, Stability, Maturity

Agates are a stone in the quartz family, they come in a variety of colors and are made of visually stunning layers of banded chalcedony. A low intensity, slow vibrating stone that works to balance oneself and steel ones reserves for an upcoming challenge by promoting stability and balance. Agate also promotes what we consider to be the mothering aspect of the goddess, aiding in developing a mature state of mind. As one would expect this stone is often used during pregnancy to decrease anxiety and prepare the mother for the role she has been gifted.

Carry Agate with you when you need to tackle something that involves a mature, level-headed, pragmatic mindset. Meditate with it to promote growth and maturity. Wear Agate as a necklace to aid in lactation and keep the stone with you during your pregnancy to promote healthy growth.

Agate has a stabilizing effect to the entire aura, transforming and eliminating negative energies. This cleansing effect is applicable to all chakras.

Almandine Garnet

Stone of Tangible Truth

Almandine, most commonly referred to as almandine garnet or simply garnet, is the most common stone in the garnet family. When you think of garnet you're most likely thinking of this dark red (sometimes) translucent stone. Almandine is a stone of healing that can aid in the regeneration of physical and mental strength, especially regarding circulation.

These properties give it the ability to not only aid in heart health but also greatly assist in enhancing sexual libido, as a lot of those issues arise from problems with circulation. Almandine is known as the "Stone of Tangible Truth" due to its ability to assist in manifestation, for the uninitiated this means it can help us in making dreams and desires become reality through affirmation, focus, and action.

Carry Almandine Garnet with you need to be at peak performance, if you're running a marathon or taking an important exam consider wearing a ring that houses this magnificent stone. A great place for this stone to be displayed is the bedroom, for obvious reasons. Meditating with almandine can have excellent regenerative properties, place near your root chakra for grounding purposes and to enhance libido.

Amazonite

Stone of Truth and Courage

Amazonite is a silicate stone that is normally a pale green in color but can range from a turquoise blue to a yellowish green, it's also commonly known as "Amazon Stone" and "Amazon Jade". This stone has the ability to assist you in speaking your mind by calming your chakras and balancing your masculine and feminine energies to eliminate anxiety and fear of judgment. Amazonite reacts strongly with the throat and heart chakras lending to its ability to assist us in communication and is also known for it's healing properties regarding the throat due to this reaction. Amazonite is also associated with good luck and prosperity and for this reason it is often used to create luck amulets and sachets.

Carry this stone with you when you have a job interview coming up, its balancing properties will help you keep a cool head under pressure when you need to vocalize your thoughts in a professional way. This stone is also a good choice if you need to have a difficult conversation with a close friend or family member about something that's been troubling you. For example, this stone could be very helpful when trying to convince a family member to get help for a mental health or addiction issue, it will help you collect your thoughts and word them in a way that doesn't anger them or leave them feeling insulted. Another use, although novel, is utilizing amazonite when playing a game of chance (like monopoly) although some might consider this cheating!

Amethyst
Stone of Sobriety and Creativity

Amethyst is a translucent purple stone in the quartz family that has been prized throughout antiquity for its breath taking appearance and mystical properties. The name of this stone is taken from the Greek "amethustos" meaning "not intoxicated"

which has led to it being commonly known as a stone of sobriety.

Amethyst is a high frequency stone that is capable of enhancing your meditative state, it stimulates the third eye chakra and aids in the development of intuition and mental clarity, this is why it's also known as the stone of creativity. This stone was used by ancient cultures to prevent oneself from going overboard while drinking and was thought to lessen the effects of alcohol, many ancient drinking vessels were adorned with these stones not only to prevent intoxication but also to prevent overindulgence.

Carry this stone with you to stave off impulsive urges and addictive instincts. If you have a problem with self-control and genuinely want to change your habits this stone can help in making the mental changes that need to be made and keeping that clarity of mind. Amethyst won't do all the work for you but can be a goddess-send when that expensive bag is calling from the store front or that bar down the street looks a bit too enticing. As said before, you can get great results in mental development of any sort while meditating with this stone, especially if you've found yourself in a creative slump or feel you've reached a dead end in your progress.

Amber

Radiance and Magnetism

Amber is a rare example of an organic gem, not crystal or mineral in nature. This miraculous gem was formed over millions of years as a result of the hardening of sap from ancient trees, sap that was used by the trees to protect it and heal its wounds, the life-force of nature. The color of amber can range from a dark opaque brown to a brilliant translucent yellow. Ambers numerous uses and unique properties amongst gemstones, like its light weight, electro-static properties, and ease of carving made it one of the most important trade items of the ancient world, leading amber to directly influence trade routes and the cultures affected since it was first found washed up on the shores of beaches across Europe and Asia being first official recorded in 4th century B.C.. Amber was referred to as *"electrum"* in Latin and *"elektron"* in Greek which meant shining/brilliant. The first recorded observation of people noticing electrical phenomenon came about when the Greeks noticed that when rubbed amber seemed to be able to attract other objects, which is why electricity and electrons are so named. I apologize for the history lesson, but I believe it's important to know a little about the origins and importance of this unique gem.

From a metaphysical perspective amber has long been used as protective amulet for children, either made into jewelry or faceted to their clothing. Mothers have long used amber to ease pregnancy pain and to soothe the gums of children that are teething, although it should be noted that amber when used for teething should never go into the mouth, it's best worn as jewelry on the mother or placed close to a child but not within their reach. Since amber is the life blood and healing mechanism of the trees in which it came from it should go without saying that it has innumerable healing and restorative properties. Ambers organic nature means that it is a product of a living organism that was fueled by the power of the sun, lending to it being known throughout history as a sun stone, a gem that was produced by millions of years of energy transference starting with perhaps the most important celestial body, Helios. Amber increases natural radiance and can have magnetic properties in regard to relationships, be they platonic or romantic. The electrostatic properties of amber make it a great choice for pulling out toxins and negative energies, consider pairing it with a purifying quartz-based stone.

Carry Amber on your person when you need to radiate energy, it can be useful in any situation where you need to be the center of attention, just make sure that you're ready for the extra eyes that will be on you and make sure you're in a position to take advantage of the magnetism that comes with this gem. As said before amber can be used to ease pains associated with reproduction, including but not limited to menstrual pains, pregnancy cramps, and issues related to breast feeding. DO NOT ALLOW CHILDREN TO CHEW ON AMBER. Amber can also be used in tandem with light therapy and conventional therapy to help treat depression.

Amber stimulates the naval chakra, which is the center of your life force energies, the naval chakra being integral to decision making and other important though processes. Hold amber in your hands near your naval while meditating to help balance this chakra and help alleviate problems with focus and confusion that might arise from your naval chakra being out of balance.

Andradite Garnet

Emotional Strength and Grounding

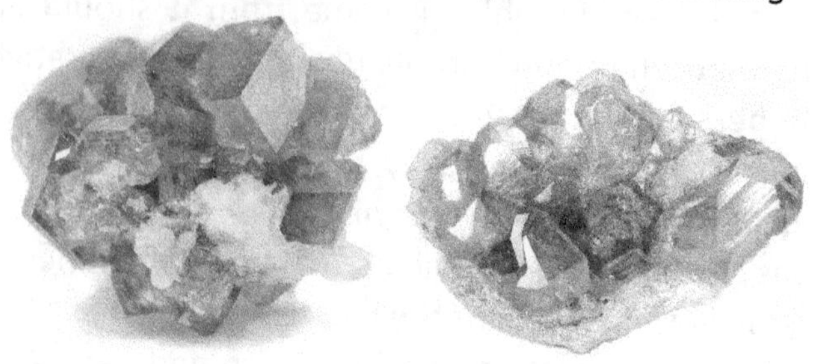

Andradite is a calcium iron silicate in the garnet family that generally has a translucent olive or yellowish-green appearance. Andradite can be further categorized in to three separate types that are characterized by their unique colors. Demantoid Andradite include various shades of olive and dark green and is considered to be the rarest and most sought-after type of andradite and is used to overcome obstacles in relationships and to lessen feelings of isolation. Melanite Andradite has a glossy black appearance and is often used for grounding purposes, melanite exudes strong positive masculine energy and encourages healthy emotional responses especially in men who have been taught to bottle up their feelings. Topazolite Andradite is yellow in color and is said to be the most active of the andradites and is useful in promoting feelings of determination and focus.

Carry this stone with you to stay grounded and encourage healthy emotional responses. You might want to use a specific type of andradite depending on your goals and circumstances.

Consider utilizing this stone if you have issues with staying on task, meditate with this stone near the solar plexus while concentrating on your relationships with other people and how you can bring more balance to those relationships.

Andradite Garnet activates the Heart Chakra which regulates our interactions with the world around us. A well-balanced Heart Chakra allows us to be ourselves around others without fear or anxiety and helps us interact with the people around us without getting overly invested in their attitudes and perspectives that we might not agree with. This can be especially helpful when having to interact with people that you might not have a choice in being around, such as at work or other community functions.

Apatite

Action and Manifestation

Apatite is a phosphate mineral gemstone that can be found in a variety of colors ranging from shades of blue and green to brilliant yellows and vibrant pinks.

Apatite is a stone of manifestation and action, especially in regard to service of others and activist pursuits, it reacts with the third eye and throat chakras and can be useful in the development of intuition and voicing your thoughts. Apatite has the ability to increase motivation and decrease complacency by stimulating the mind and driving action.

Carry this stone with you when speaking out about issues that concern you, a great stone to have when working on community projects and while participating in the political process. Meditate with this stone to spur action and motivation, place it near the crown chakra to promote mental/psychic activity and near the throat to encourage rhetorical prowess.

Aquamarine
Safe Travels and Calm Resolve

Aquamarine is a pale-blue to light-green stone in the beryl family. Aquamarine is named after the Latin word for sea water.

It was commonly used by sailors to protect them from harsh waves and weather and was thought to have the power to calm storms. Aquamarine is also known as the stone of youth, carried by anyone who wished to hold on to their vitality. Aquamarine reacts with the throat chakra and can be used by teachers or anyone with a public speaking job to calm your thoughts and nerves.

Carry aquamarine with you when you need to stay calm in the presence of large groups of people, it can be extremely effective for academics and students that have presentation anxiety. Consider giving a child that's learning to swim a necklace or ring that's faceted with this stone. Meditate with this stone near the throat chakra to encourage confidence in speaking and presentation.

Aventurine

Leadership and Decisiveness

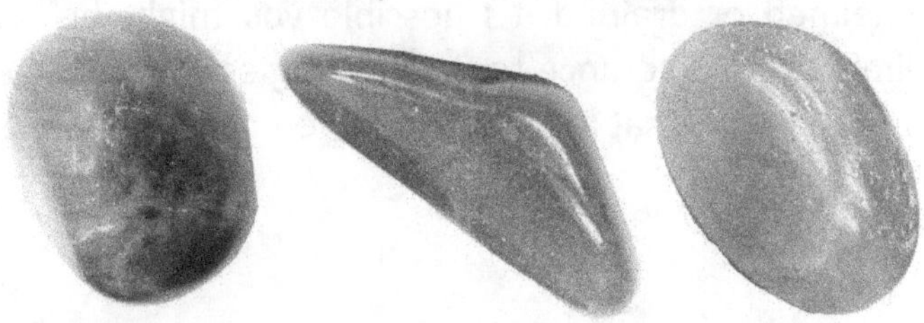

Aventurine is a stone in the quartz family characterized by its inclusion of platy minerals that give it a unique shimmering effect called aventurescence. Aventurine comes in a variety of colors with green being the most common, the color of aventurine is determined by the type of mineral inclusions in the stone.

This stone promotes good leadership qualities, can be helpful in the process of decision making and can spur action amongst stagnation. The green variety activates the heart chakra, the blue the crown chakra, and the red activates the root. This stone can be used with its corresponding chakras to encourage positive growth and development. For example, blue aventurine can be used in a similar way as amethyst for the development of intuition by working with the crown chakra.

Carry this stone with you when you need to take charge, if the situation calls for logical problem solving use the blue stone, if it's an issue that will come with heavy emotional strain use the green, if you're heading into a situation that is already out of control and you'd like to bring balance and a grounded direction consider using the red stone. These stones can also be used together if the need arises but be sure that you're able to withstand the amount of energy these combined crystals will be giving off. Experiment at home before jumping into the fray equipped with a veritable infinity gauntlet, you should be able to gauge your own tolerance by carrying the stones around the house while going about your daily routine. If you feel overwhelmed or drained it's possible you might be pushing your limits. Your tolerance to these energies will increase with time so test yourself at a rate in which you're comfortable with.

Azurite

Enlightenment and Memory

Azurite is a dark blue copper mineral that is created by the result of weathering copper ore deposits. This stone resonates at the exact frequency of the third eye chakra and has been prized since antiquity for its ability to promote enlightened thinking and memory retention. Scholars, priests, and royalty throughout history are said to have utilized this powerful stone. Azurite was known as the "Stone of Heaven" by the ancient Chinese and they believed it had the power to open celestial gateways. Other ancient civilizations such as the Romans and Mayans used Azurite for similar purposes, all connected by their understanding of this stones potential to open up our minds to the spiritual plane.

Carry this stone with you whenever your memory needs to be at peak performance, a great stone to work with if you need to memorize information for a presentation or remember key parts of a project to reference back to. While there are many practical uses for this stone the most obvious use is that of seeking enlightenment and alignment with the spirit world. While stones like amethyst resonate with the third eye chakra to enhance clairvoyance and perceptions, this stone is best used to connect with the ethereal for purposes of enlightenment and introspection.

Bloodstone (Heliotrope)

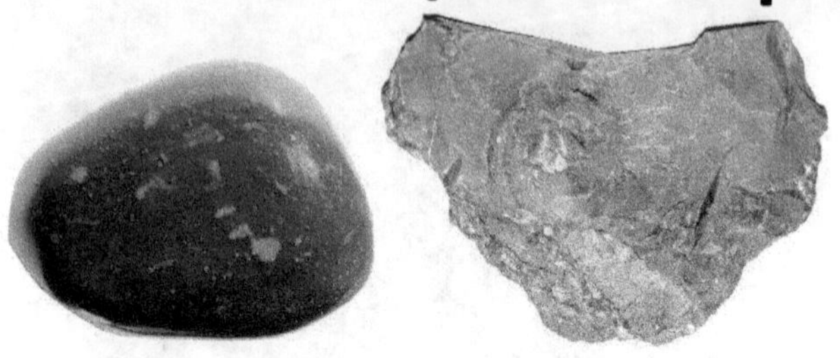

Most Bloodstones are generally solid dark-green jasper with red hematite inclusions although the inclusions may sometimes occur in chalcedony. It was a common practice for Roman soldier to carry this stone as it was said to have the power to staunch bleeding, bloodstone is still used in some parts of the world that practice homeopathic medicine, such as India, for the purposes a purifying blood and healing wounds. The iron-oxide contained in the stone that give it its bloody appearance is likely the cause as it's a powerful astringent that causes blood vessels to constrict potentially helping with blood loss.

There are numerous records from historians from late antiquity about this important stone, for the sake of brevity I'll only list a few. Pliny the Elder in the first century who first noted that magicians of the age were taking interest in the stone for its potential to be used for amulets of invisibility. Damigeron in the 4th century noted that the stone was known to have the ability to influence the weather and preserve youth and vitality. The Greeks, who called the stone "heliotrope" (Sun Stone) used the stone to help in farming and to cleanse the blood of venoms and the Gnostics of the first century wore the stone as an amulet of longevity. A running theme within the history of this stone is life, whether it was used for healing and preserving life that was being threatened or used to ensure a good harvest this stone excels in radiating life energy.

Carry this stone with you as a protective amulet, especially useful for people in the nursing, hospice, or any general healthcare profession. Carry this stone with you while camping to ward off venomous insects and reptiles. Bloodstone is a powerful detoxifier and can be used cleanse the body and mind of toxins and impurities, meditate with the stone between the root and heart chakras to realign and cleanse your energies. Heliotrope is also an ideal stone for situations where you need to be at the top of your game physically, such as going to the gym, running a marathon, or any activity that involves physical endurance.

Blue Chalcedony
The Stone of Speech

Blue Chalcedony, also referred to as "blue chrysoprase" is a bluish form of silica that is composed of fine intergrowths of moganite and quartz. The stone has a waxy luster and is often translucent or semitransparent. Chalcedony is mentioned in several ancient texts ranging from Pliny the Elder's "Naturalis

Historia" to Revelations in the Christian Bible. It's believed that the name of the stone likely comes from the town "Chalcedon" in modern Turkey. Ceremonial knives made of chalcedony have been found in Australia dating back 32,000 years and Chalcedony was commonly used in ring facets, seals, beads and other jewelry as far back as 1800 BC.

Blue Chalcedony stimulates the throat chakra and is often used for purposes relating to the voice. It's also a stone of balance and help regulate and balance the other chakras as well. Stimulation of the throat chakras can help in channeling energy from the lower chakras by giving your energies a clear and stable path. First and foremost, blue chalcedony is a stone of communication and is very useful in anything that has to do with oration, meditating with chalcedony can help alleviate anxieties relating to having a difficult conversation or a tryout/interview. Chalcedony also promotes optimistic thinking and aids us in speaking out truth, however difficult it may be.

Cacoxenite

Stone of Acension

Cacoxenite is an iron aluminium phosphate mineral which is common associated with iron ore but can also be found as inclusions within quartz and amethyst and generally appears as a yellowish, gold, or earth brown color. The name cacoxenite comes from the Greek word for "evil" or "bad" due to the phosphorus content lessening the quality of iron made from ore that contains the mineral. While cacoxenite has historically caused issues in smelting iron from ore its magical properties cannot be understated.

Cacoxenite is known as the "Stone of Ascension" and can raise spiritual awareness and understanding. This stone has the ability to rejuvenate the spirit and dispel doubts about your place in the world and cosmos. Cacoxenite can help us connect to the spirit and bring forth new and undiscovered thoughts and talents and can eliminate thoughts of doubt or limitation.

Cacoxenite vibrates at a very high frequency and is useful in increasing spiritual awareness and aligning the third chakra, it can help us mute our inner monologue and listen to the goddess/spirit. Cacoxenite encourages positive and "outside the box" thinking and can be a great stone to use to help with the creative process. When this stone is used with or is an inclusion in amethyst it can aid in opening and focusing the crown chakra which can greatly aid in psychic protection from negative thoughts and energies. This stone is often used for emotional healing, creating a space to withdraw and overcome fear and stress.

Carnelian

The Singers Stone

Carnelian is generally orange or reddish in color and is a variety of the silica mineral chalcedony and is colored by impurities of iron oxide. The name carnelian is thought to either come from the Latin word for flesh or from the Latin word "cornum" which is the name of the reddish "cornel cherry". While carnelian is mostly known for its striking orange hues it can also present as a very pale orange to a darker almost black hue. Carnelian has been found all around the world and has been used throughout antiquity by a plethora of ancient societies, from jewelry adorning the breastplates of the Hebrew High Priests to art dating back to 1800 BC. Carnelian was used to during Roman times to make signet and seal rings for imprinting seals onto documents of importance as the hot wax used for the seals would not stick to the carnelian. Carnelian is also mentioned in Revelations, a book of the Christian Bible, as a stone that is part of the foundation of the heavenly city walls.

Carnelian is a stone of leadership, courage, and empowerment. It can invigorate and bring back energy lost through tribulation and the daily drain that comes with work and dealing with life's stresses. This stone can alleviate negative feelings of jealousy in relationships and is especially helpful in dealing with sexual insecurities. Carnelian can promote healthy blood flow and stimulate the metabolism lending to its ability to help with sexual issues.

The Sacral Chakra is associated with this stone as it's invigorating properties can spark sexual desire and passion, it stimulates this chakra and can unblock the pathways that might lead to impotence and low libido. Meditate with this stone while holding it near the Sacral Chakra (below the naval) to aid in the restoration of lost vitality, concentrate on the issues at hand and visualize renewed lifeforce flowing through your veins and the extremities of your body.

Celestite

The Stone of Heavenly Communication

Celestite is a mineral consisting of strontium sulfate and is generally a pale blue color but can also be found in white and orange varieties. This stone is found all around the world with the most popular pale-blue variety being mostly found in

Madagascar. Celestite gets its name from the Latin word "caelestis" which means "celestial", which is derived from the Latin word "caelum" which means "sky" or "heaven".

Celestite is useful in communicating with heavenly spirits by opening a pathway that is free from material blockage. It does this by clearing our auras of negative energies and thoughts such as anxiety, apprehension, and other fears that bring about a chaotic mind state. This stone is a great aid in pre-meditation rituals to cleanse your aura and prepare your body to be receptive to heavenly communication. Celestite is also a great stone for creatives and can be placed in an art room or space where creativity is paramount. Celestite has a radiant energy that stimulates the throat chakra and allows the energies from other chakras to be expressed which is helpful in speaking truth in difficult situations and can also be helpful in activating the crown and brow chakras.

Celestite is a stone of trust, responsibility, and patience and can help to solidify a bond with heavenly bodies, such as the goddess, and can be used in communing and revering your ancestral/angelic guides. Use this stone to balance the upper chakras allowing for optimal communication of all kinds, but as stated before, especially with communication pertaining to the spirit world.

Charoite

The Stone of Transformation

Charoite is an extremely rare silicate mineral that is only found in one known location, the Sakha Republic in Siberia. Charoite is a pearly translucent purple with an unusual fibrous, swirling appearance. The name charoite comes from the Russian word "chary" which means "magic" or "charm" This stone was first discovered in the early 20th century and isn't known to be recorded in any historical documents.

The energies of this stone offer a unique synthesis of the heart and crown chakras which brings forth feeling of unconditional love which is grounded on the material plane. This stone has the ability to allow us to let go of transgressions and negative feelings we have towards others. Charoite can help guide us down our spiritual path and is especially helpful to those just starting out on their journey of self-discovery and awakening, it helps in nurturing our altruistic side and can help in empathizing with and understanding others point of view while dealing with the potential contradictions and dissonance caused by these differences in understanding.

Charoite is believed to help with blood flow and is known to alleviate the symptoms of ADHD with its calming energies. It has also been reported to help with cramping, headaches, high blood pressure and can assist with insomnia or other sleep-related problems.

Chrysocolla

The Stone of Communication

Chrysocolla is a mineral that's makeup isn't completely understood but is thought to be a mixture of copper hydroxide spertiniite and chalcedony. The name comes from ancient Greek "chrysos" and "kolla" meaning "gold" and "glue" which comes from the fact that it was used to solder gold, notably by Theophrastus in 315 BC. Chrysocolla is blueish-green in color (cyan) and is a minor ore of copper and forms in the oxidation zones of copper ore.

Chrysocolla is fairly common and is frequently used in jewelry due to its wide availability, striking color, and its ease of shaping. While chrysocolla comes in a variety of blue hues, the lighter blue-green colors are most often used due to the darker blues being too soft to work with.

Chrysocolla is a stone of communication, expression, and empowerment. The calming color of this stone contributes to its ability to help us relay our thoughts and knowledge with understanding and empathy, a great stone for teachers or anyone in the profession of conveying information to others. This stone also makes a great talisman for musicians or anyone in need of putting our thoughts into words by calming our chaotic thoughts into a cohesive stream of information.

Chrysocolla can open the throat chakra allowing for clear and concise communication and can help us to not only speak with knowledge but with wisdom. This stone is also especially useful in earth-grounding and can be a great aid when attempting astral travel.

Citrine

The Merchant's Stone

Citrine is a pale-yellow stone that is a variety of quartz, the yellow coloring is caused by submicroscopic distribution of colloidal ferric hydroxide impurities. Citrine's name is derived from the Latin word "citrina" which simply means "yellow" and is the origin of the word citron. Citrine has been referred to as "The Merchant's Stone" or "The Money Stone" due to a belief held for thousands of years that this stone has the ability to attract wealth.

Citrine is a transmuter and grounder of negative energies and works well as a home protection crystal, helping to not only absorb negative energies directed at the home but helping resolve issues that might arise within it. Citrine, along with kyanite, is one of few crystals that don't need to be cleansed or cleared due to these transmutational properties. Citrine is a stone of manifestation and willpower, resonating with the energies of the Sun and shares in its ability to encourage energetic, vigorous action.

Citrine works with the solar plexus and sacral chakras, opening and energizing our centers of vitality. It stimulates the life forces of the body and helps them function as a sort of magnet to our desires and ambitions. Promotes our awareness of the universal life force and is extremely useful in manifestation of our goals which is why it has always been known as a promoter and attracter of wealth. Citrine is also said to have healing properties in terms of digestion and pancreatic health, it's also good for promoting healthy skin, hair, and nails. From an emotional perspective citrine is known to have the power to overcome fear, negative thoughts, and destructive feelings.

Dalmatian Jasper

The Stone of Playful Energy

Dalmatian Jasper, contrary to the name, isn't actually a type of Jasper but a form of the igneous rock Perthite. The dots that lend to this stones name are composed of rare amphibole arfvedsonite but is commonly misunderstood to contain tourmaline. The stone ranges in color from a pale grey to a cream/beige color with very dark, usually black, spots.

Dalmatian Jasper promotes a positive and jovial outlook and can be particularly helpful when trying to tackle a problem from a different perspective. This stone promotes emotional harmony and helps us keep perspective when dealing with emotionally draining issues. Dalmatian Jasper encourages positive team outcomes and helps us see the bright side of things when the chaos of working with others seems overwhelming. It's also known to be the stone of pets, especially dogs, and can be helpful in creating a bond and trust between you and your furry friends.

Dalmatian Jasper is known for it's healing properties related to joint, tendon, and muscle health and its slow emitting energies help open up the base, earth and sacral chakras. It's resonation with the base chakras promote balance and overall strength and stamina while rekindling our jovial energies which can be especially helpful in leadership positions that require positivity and balanced thoughts. The attitudes this stone promotes is necessary for accumulating and propagating wisdom in a way that is attractive to ourselves and those around us.

Diamond

The Stone of Resilience

Diamonds are made of carbon with its atoms arranged in a crystal structure, this crystal has the highest thermal conductivity and hardness of any natural material known to man. These properties make diamonds a very sought after and useful material in regard to its industrial uses and people around the world love diamonds for their beauty and the symbolism associated with them.

Diamonds act as an amplifier and conductor of energy, taking in our thoughts, feelings, desires and radiating them outwards with an unmatched brilliance. The healing properties of diamonds cannot be overstated, it is one of the most effective purifiers of the mind diand helps with brain function and creativity. Diamonds have been used for millennia for a wide range of reasons, it is thought to help with cognitive abilities and to prevent the effects of aging by promoting cell regeneration and decreasing impurities in the body.

It should be noted that diamonds should not be always used for every situation, especially when in a bad mind state due to its ability to amplify those negative emotions. It's best to use other stones paired with meditation to achieve the state of mind that we wish to have and then using diamonds to amplify and strengthen those feelings.

Diamonds have the unique ability to open up all of the chakras with an emphasis on the Crown and Etheric Chakras with its high-frequency energies. This notable crystal is especially useful in achieving a state of mind that is conducive to connecting us with higher planes of existence and allowing us to be receptive of cosmic messages and lessons.

Diamonds are symbolic of resilience and strength and are commonly used in ritual bonding ceremonies such as marriage but can also be used for a myriad of other things such as the blessing of a new home, giving it protection that the hardened nature of this stone provides.

Emerald

The Stone of Truth and Love

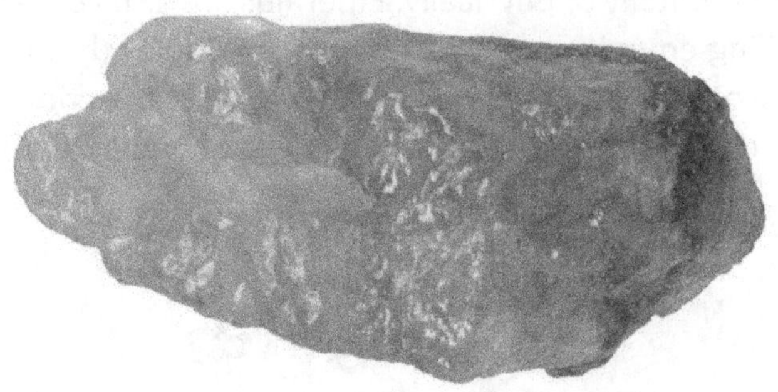

Emerald is a variety of Beryl that has been colored green by small amounts of vanadium and chromium. The word emerald is derived from the Latin word "Esmaralda "which means "green gem". The Egyptians prized this green gemstone and used it to craft jewelry and would commonly bury high ranking officials with the stone for protection during the journey to the afterlife. The lithologist St. Hildegard of Bingen once stated "All the green of nature is concentrated within the Emerald" and it has been a prized stone around the world for its beauty for over 6 thousand years. It is considered to be one of the 4 "precious" gemstones along with ruby, diamond, and sapphire.

Emeralds are associated with the Heart Chakra, the soothing energies of the emerald nurtures patience, understanding, and unconditional love. Emeralds promote friendship, equality in relationships and is known for its ability to provide cohesion and fidelity in domestic life. This gemstone is especially helpful in reigniting passion in a marriage or relationship that has dulled with the passing of time, but it can also be used for reigniting passions associated with professions and hobbies.

Emeralds have unmatched rejuvenating qualities and is not only great for the rejuvenation of the mind and relationships but also for the body, especially the heart. Meditate with an emerald whenever you are feeling fatigued or burnt out, whether mentally or physically. Emeralds are also very effective in instilling empathy and compassion for things that might be difficult otherwise, use it to foster your connection to the Divine Love to achieve heightened levels of understanding and cohesion.

Fire Agate

The Stone of Passion

Fire Agate is a variety of chalcedony that is only found in Meso-America, specifically Central and Northern Mexico and the Southwestern United States. The fiery visuals produced by Fire Agate is caused by the "Schiller Effect" which is also what causes the iridescent effect of mother-of-pearl. This happens due to alternating iron-oxide and silica layers which diffract light causing interference, this leads to the fiery effect the stone is known for.

Fire Agate is a stone of action and passion, this stone was formed from volcanic activity and carries with it those fiery energies. When life is in a lull and it seems that you're at a dead end this stone can help you put a spark back in your step, igniting your lost passions and inspiring you to think outside the box to blaze new pathways. Fire Agate can also be helpful in your love life, invigorating the lower Chakras and kindling new flames in a tired relationship.

Fire Agate can be worn as jewelry to help with energy levels and can restore lost vitality, it's especially useful in work that can be emotionally and physically draining, renewing ambition and purpose. This stone is also a protector, shielding us from those draining energies. While Fire Agate can help us rekindle desire for the things we care about, it can also be used to quell desires for things that we wish to no longer care for such as addiction and self-destructive activities.

Fire Agate stimulates the Base/Root Chakra, the center of spiritual and physical energy. This Chakra governs action, movement, and stability. It also has the ability to stabilize your aura and cleanse the entire body of negative energies with its stabilizing effects.

Fluorite

The Stone of Soothing

Fluorite is calcium fluoride in mineral form, pure fluorite is transparent and colorless but it typically has impurities that give it a wide range of colors. The word fluorite is a Latin verb meaning "to flow", due to its properties that make it useful in iron smelting as a flux, decreasing the viscosity of slag. The modern term fluorescence comes from this stones ability to absorb short wave-length light and emit it as long wave-length light. Fluorite also has many scientific applications including but not limited to a very effective lens material for microscopes and telescopes.

Fluorite is a stone of mental clarity and serenity, it is one of the most effective stones at absorbing and transmuting negative energies such as guilt, feelings of regret, anxiety, confusion, fear, and depression. It takes in these energies and emits them back to us transformed in slow, calm waves. Fluorite can also decrease the negative effects of electronic fields and is especially useful to people working around electronics such as computers and industrial machines.

Fluorite is commonly shaped into eggs, angels and spheres with the intention of breaking down the barriers between our world and the spiritual plane. The energies from Fluorite stimulate the Crown Chakra which is our gateway to the heavens and extra-spatial reality. This stone is extremely helpful in developing and opening the third eye, allowing us to perceive which others can not and manifesting the universal will onto the material plane. Fluorite is one of the best stones to use during meditation and spiritual exploration, it has been known to produce insights and visions that can answer questions we might not have thought to ask, fluorite pyramids are especially useful in meditation as it is symbolic of the soul's evolution towards a higher state of being.

Fuchsite

The Stone of Tough Love

Fuchsite is a chromium variety of the muscovite mineral. An aluminum atom in muscovite is replaced with a chromium atom giving the stone its distinctive apple-green hue. Fuchsite has fluorescent properties and emits lime-green light waves under

UV light and has an extremely small amount of radioactivity (don't worry it's completely safe).

Fuchsite is capable of remedying the most toxic of situations through realization. Many of the problems in our lives are due to factors that we sometimes turn a blind eye to or ignore in hopes of them getting better, Fuchsite has the ability to make us painfully aware of those things while giving us the motivation and care to see things strait. This is especially helpful in relationships, be they friendships, romantic partners, or co-workers. Sometimes those relationships can get into a rut due to toxicity and other negative emotions and energies, Fuchsite can bring those problems to light so they may be properly addressed.

This stone can help us see abuse and the root causes of it, it will help you be resilient in situations that don't seem to have a way out. Fuchsite won't immediately fix those situations, but the aura created by the fluorescent properties of this stone can help us grow into a person that doesn't accept our place within a negative institution. The lessons realized through the use of Fuchsite will stay with you and prepare you for whatever life has to throw at you.

Fuchsite is a stone of the Heart Chakra, it can serve as a bridge to from the mind to the heart. This stone can help us navigate difficult interactions that we might face in our day to day lives with empathy and understanding even when we might have substantial disagreements without compromising our own values and beliefs.

Garnet

The Stone of Health

Garnet is a silicate mineral that comes in a range of different chemical compositions. While the word Garnet comes from the middle-english word "gernet" meaning "dark red", garnets actually come in a variety of colors while the well known dark red variety are the most common. Garnets can be translucent or opaque, the former are commonly used for ornamentation and jewelry while the later being used for industrial purposes, mostly as an abrasive.

Garnet has been a prized stone since the times of ancient Egypt and is one of the twelve gemstones in the breastplate of the Hebrew High Priest, Native Americans have also treasured this sacred stone for millennia.

Garnet is most well known for its abilities to purify the blood and reduce toxins in our bodies. It has impressive regenerative abilities and stimulates the metabolism while repairing and regenerating DNA. These cellular regenerative properties not only improve our physical well-being but our emotional states as well and medicine men have used garnet to treat depression and alleviate patients of bad dreams. Garnet has the ability to change our mind-states for the better, countering defeatist attitudes brought about through trauma and extreme stress. When all else seems lost Garnet can help you see pathways to victory that your emotional state might have prevented you from realizing.

Garnet can invigorate the Chakras, revitalizing and balancing the energies that can be disrupted during our day-to-day challenges. It can evoke love and devotion and balance energies relating to the sex-drive and emotional disharmony. Garnet stimulates both the crown and base chakras which provides a free flow of energy through the spine and is therefore known for its healing abilities in regard to neural and spinal health.

Goldstone

The Stone of Abundance and Creation

While not a natural stone, Goldstone's usage has been widespread throughout Europe and Persia for at least 800 years and is a common stone used by practitioners of many spiritual disciplines worldwide. This manmade glass stone has been referred to by many names such as "monkstone" due to its folkloric associations with an unnamed monastic group, "aventurine glass" and "del-roba" which is Persian for "charming". The flecks of "gold" in the stone is created by the inclusion of iron or copper flecks during the manufacturing process. The bulk of the stone is generally made of Gypsum and Feldspar.

Goldstone is a stone of creation and abundance; it helps us channel our thoughts into real world applications. It's a stone of change and alchemy, representing progressive positive steps in creating the realities we wish to inhabit. This "charming" stone can be worn while trying to foster new relationships, whether they be romantic or plutonic, creating a positive aura that facilitates new beginnings.

Due to it being a man-made glass that is highly reflective, Goldstone can be used as a protective amulet that reflects negativity and harmful energies. In ancient times this stone would be placed in window seals to protect the owners from malicious intent and evil spirits. Goldstone is also said to be great for circulation and joint health while granting the courage and ambition needed to get the things you want out of life, shaping your ideal reality.

Goshenite Beryl

The Stone of Motherhood

Goshenite is the purist form of Beryl and is commonly found inside of Granite. It is commonly referred to as "The Mother of all Gemstones" due to the fact that it can be transformed into other gemstones such as morganite, emerald, aquamarine and bixbite, which are gemstones that are impure forms of Beryl that are colored by various trace amounts of elements such as chromium or vanadium.

Goshenite is a feminine crystal of the moon and angels that has long been associated with motherhood. Its high frequencies resonate with the frequency of truth that helps promote fidelity, honor, loyalty, and respect. Goshenite has been used since antiquity for matters associated with vision and truth, it has been used in magnifying glasses, early eyeglasses and has been placed on the eyelids at night to improve eyesight.

Goshenite has impressive metaphysical properties, it has the ability to open the Etheric and Crown Chakras and stimulate mental acuity. It's a stone of mental clarity that can prevent us from falling prey to deception and ill-intent. In meditation it can be used to sharpen our creative abilities and help us give birth to new and constructive ideas. Used in conjunction with other Beryl stones it has the ability to strengthen and enhance their energies.

Goshenite can help us when dealing with maternal struggles, it can bring serenity to women in labor or going through pregnancy pains, it can help us deal with unruly children and give single mothers the resolve to take on the challenges that come with the raising of children. Goshenite can also help with menstrual problems and issues that arise with menopause. Goshenite is particularly useful in inducing dream states that promote vivid and lucid dreaming.

Heliodor

The Stone of The Sun

Heliodor is a variety of Beryl that ranges in color from yellow to light green to brown. The yellow tint of this stone is attributed to the ferric ions within the Beryl. The name Heliodor is Greek for "gift of the Sun".

Heliodor provides relief from immense burdens and pressure; it gives us the radiant power needed to face even the most difficult of struggles. Heliodor provides hope and a pathway to reacquiring things that have been lost, whether they be physical or spiritual. It's also a stone of persuasion, guiding us down the path needed to resolve conflict and have things turn out in our favor. Heliodor can also be useful in memory retention and is a great stone to aid in research and study. Place a Heliodor stone in a sunny window seal to amplify the Suns radiant empowering energies throughout your home.

Heliodor energies focus at the Solar Plexus Chakra and allows one to channel their inner energies and manifest them into physical realities. The Solar Plexus Chakra is our center for energy distribution and can lead to overall health and wellness, when our energies are in balance at the solar plexus we have the power to interpret things clearly and make powerful and concise decisions. Heliodor also works in tandem with the crown chakra to provide peace and oneness. Heliodor can also strengthen the immune system, the power of the sun can help us avoid contaminates and impurities that we come into contact with on a daily basis, negating their negative influence.

This stone is helpful to those who have suffered abuse and can help us reclaim our power and stability, giving us confidence and restoring our trust in ourselves. It allows us to set aside the fear and doubt that we have harbored and take back what is rightfully ours, a life full of growth, renewal and strength. It can help us to see the world as it is and to see through the manipulative forces that keep us from living our truth.

Hematite

The Blood Stone

Hematite is an iron oxide crystal compound that is commonly found around the world in both rocks and soil. It is electrically conductive and presents in a variety of colors including black, steel, brown, grey, silver and red. The name Hematite comes from the Greek word "haima" which means "blood" due to the red coloration often found in the stone due to the oxidization of the iron that make up this stones properties. Hematite has been used for thousands of years for decorative purposes, it was also used to craft weapons and armor as its dark color was perceived to be intimidating and protective.

Hematite is frequently associated with Mars, the god of war and battle, it is said to offer protective auras from physical and mental attack. Although the imagery of war and battle would typically evoke feelings of pain and hardships Hematite is a nurturing stone, it leads us down a path of trials and tribulations and lifts us up so that we may conquer all that stand before us, wishing us harm. While Hematite will present us with difficulties that might seem insurmountable it will never give us more than we can handle, its intention being one of growth and expansion of the soul. It will help us confront the darkest parts of our spirits and see them for what they are, putting our souls through a crucible that will give us the resolve needed to achieve our dreams.

Hematite is especially helpful to those with ADHD and anxiety as it can help us stay on task and have a goal-oriented mindset. Hematite jewelry is common and very popular for this reason, it helps us take what we're thinking and articulate it in a way that is easy to understand and digest. If you have stage/presentation fright Hematite will help calm your mind so that you can properly formulate your ideas and present them in a way that others are more likely to understand and accept.

Hematite is also one of the best stones for absorbing negative energies. If you're having issues sleeping or with bad dreams, try placing a piece of hematite under your pillow at night. If your home is plagued with negative energies or spirits place hematite around the house in doors and window seals to catch any negative energies that might try to make their way into your home.

Hematite resonates with the root chakra and can help keep us grounded to reality by giving an out to all the negative energies that we take on in our day to day lives. It can help bring about balance when dealing with stressful situations and can be a great stone to use when making important decisions that require you to take multiple factors while maintaining your sense of self and your value-system.

Jade

Jade actually refers to two different kinds of silicate minerals: Nephrite (a silicate of magnesium and calcium) and Jadeite (a silicate of aluminum and sodium) and can come in a variety of colors with green being the most well-known. The two minerals are nearly indistinguishable and can only be differentiated by the sound the stone makes when struck. Jade is most well known for its usage in Asian art and medicine but also has a rich history of usage in ancient Meso and South American cultures as well.

In Ancient China Jade was plentiful and used to craft many common and ceremonial items and was known as the Imperial Gem as far back as 8,000 years ago. Everyday decorative items were commonly carved from Jade, notably the mouthpieces of pipes as they believed that breathing through Jade could increase the length of ones life. It was also common for people of high status to be buried with trinkets of Jade, the wealthiest would often be buried inside of suits made entirely of Jade and Gold. Jade is the national stone of Japan and has been made into bracelets to show power and wealth, Jade was also commonly used in rituals and it was believed the green stone enabled fertility, longevity, and would strengthen the soul. Jade has also been used in many other various cultures across the world for thousands of years including India, Korea, and Mesoamerica where it was an extremely rare and prized stone that would be used for various religious practices and hieroglyphics.

Jade is a powerful stone of healing, especially regarding organ health, this has been known for thousands of years and has led to some referring to Jade as "The Spleen Stone". Jade can help speed up recovery times after surgery and promote overall organ health and function through the cleansing and purification of toxins that hinder our bodily functions. The restorative properties of Jade also extend to other parts of the body and is believed to speed up the process of healing from injured joints, muscles and bones, likely due to its purifying nature.

Jade might be most well known for its ability to attract success and wealth, meditate with Jade when trying to make difficult decisions about money, such as investments or career paths. These prosperous energies have been used for millennia by many a merchant and lord to promote clear and levelheaded decisions that lead to the best outcomes in any given situation, no matter the murkiness of your options. Practitioners of Feng Shui place jade in the southeast corner of a home or workplace to bring wealth and good fortune. A stone of the Heart Chakra, this stone can be helpful in contributing to your overall emotional well-being especially in regard to dealing with monetary decision making.

Jasper

The Stone of Tranquility

Jasper is an opaque variety of quartz or chalcedony, it's an impure variety of silica that can present in nearly any color, often a combination of several colors. In ancient times the name Jasper was used to refer to a variety of different stones, some being translucent, but today we general only refer to the opaque varieties as Jasper. The Jasper that was referred to in ancient texts was likely Nephrite or Chalcedony. The name Jasper is from the Old French word "Jaspre" which means "spotted stone".

Jasper has strong powers of stabilization and alignment, place Jasper on the Base Chakra and move it up the Chakra points one by one to realign and cleanse the entire Chakra system. The stabilizing powers of Jasper can be used to achieve an unparalleled sense of tranquility and jewelry fashioned from Jasper can be extremely useful in chaotic situations and environments.

Jaspers unique composition of many different minerals make it especially useful in tuning oneself with the energies of the Earth and can help you ground and sync yourself with the vibrations of nature. These grounding forces can impart a serenity that enables you to touch base with reality and put things into perspective, it's especially useful when you're about to embark into unknown territory, whether that be literally through travel or when starting a new job or relationship.

Jasper is believed to have many health benefits, especially in regard to balancing and regulating the bodies mineral content, balancing your supply of sulfur, iron, zinc, and manganese. Jasper water (created by placing a jasper stone in any vessel of water) can be helpful to the digestive system and indirectly to organ health.

Kyanite

The Bridgeway Stone

Kyanite is an aluminum silicate mineral that can range in color from pale blue to dark blue. The name Kyanite comes from the Greek word for "kyanos" meaning "dark blue" which is where we get the word "cyan" from. Kyanite was first discovered in 1789 and has been used for a variety of purposes such as the manufacturing of electronic parts, ceramics, abrasives and it also functions as an effective electronic insulator.

Kyanite acts as a type of bridge between pathways in the mind. It can reveal abilities and levels of understanding that were previously unknown to us. This stone vibrates at an extremely high and rapid rate and can align all the chakras, it has the ability to restore the bodies store of qi and create a calming effect throughout the spirit and body, black kyanite is especially useful at clearing up blocked chakras.

Kyanite is an introspective stone that can help us analyze and understand our selves, it encourages the development of emotional maturity and ability to accept hard truths. It can help us understand our purpose and place in the world and accept those truths even if we might not be immediately receptive to these revelations. Kyanite encourages loyalty and fair treatment and can be helpful in situations where conflict and disagreement are likely to occur, it helps us understand others positions and approach them in a way that won't be misunderstood or easily dismissed.

Kyanite helps us find our way when everything seems to be stagnant, encouraging change and the pursuit of new ideas and emotions. Having kyanite on us, whether in our pockets or as a piece of jewelry can help us sharpen our communication skills and express ourselves in a way that promotes understanding and empathy, bridging the gap between seemingly impossible situations.

Labradorite

The Stone of Shielding

Labradorite is a calcium enriched feldspar mineral that often displays an iridescent effect. The name comes from the town where Labradorite was first identified, Labrador, Canada. This stone can come in a variety of colors ranging from gray, brown, greenish, pale green, blue, yellow and can even be colorless.

There are many myths and legends associated with this stone, the most prominent of these is that the native peoples of Canada believe that the Northern Lights were produced when an Inuit warrior struck a piece of labradorite with his spear, unleashing the auroras that we see in the northern skies.

Labradorite is one of the most protective stones you can have, it acts as a shield against negative energies and vibrations that would otherwise affect your chakras causing potential misalignment. It allows us to explore the world around us with the confidence that this stone will protect us from negative influence and those that would wish to cause us harm.

Labradorite can calm an overactive mind while still stoking our imagination and can be helpful while working on projects or learning new information, it's especially helpful to those with ADHD and ADD due to its ability to help us maintain focus without stunting the creative process.

Labradorites energy stimulates the throat chakra and can help with self-expression and speaking our mind, easing doubts that we might have from fear of judgement and negativity. It's protective energy also helps us when trying to move past the veil of the void to discover more about ourselves and our past lives, astral traveling and introspective meditation can be greatly aided by the presence of this stone.

Lapis Lazuli

The Stone of Wisdom and Truth

Lapis Lazuli is a stone comprised mostly of the mineral Lazurite, it also contains sodalite, calcite, and pyrite which comprise the gold flecks found in the stone. "Lapis" is the Latin word for "stone" and "Lazuli" is taken from the Arabic word "lazaward" meaning "heaven" or "sky". Lapis Lazuli was first discovered in Afghanistan over 6000 years ago and has been long valued for its beauty and was used in expensive jewelry and in the construction of many important ancient buildings and burial sites. the most expensive dye in antiquity, known as ultramarine, was made from the ground powder of this stone and was used by many famous painters, it was also used in important religious manuscripts and is often used in paintings to color the clothes of important people, notably The Virgin Mary.

Lapis Lazuli is a stone a truth and wisdom, it encourages honesty and righteousness and is an excellent stone for those in professions that involve oration and integrity such as journalism, teaching, law, artistry and other forms of intellectual communication. It can encourage healthy conversation and debate and can help with raising and mentoring unruly children. Being a stone of wisdom, Lapis Lazuli can help bring harmony and understanding in relationships of all kinds, allowing us to couch our emotions and speak wisely from our mind and spirit.

Lapis Lazuli balances the energies of the Throat Chakra and can help activate the Third Eye Chakra. It can help us be aware of things in our environment that we might have previously overlooked, giving us new insight and understanding. This stone has the ability to elevate our consciousness to a higher plane, lifting us above our base emotional responses allowing us to think clearly and intentionally, quieting the noise that gets in the way of making wise decisions.

Malachite

A Stone of Protection and Well-Being

Malachite is a copper carbonate hydroxide mineral. This stone is generally a dark opaque green with lighter green banding. The name Malachite is derived from the Greek "molochites lithos" meaning "mallow-green stone" due to resemblance to the leaves of the mallow plant. Malachite is an ore of copper and has been mined for nearly 4000 years and smelted produce copper ingots and has also been used as an ornamental gemstone.

In the 1600s the Spanish believed that malachite had the ability to soothe an irritable child by helping keep evil spirits away. Marbodus, a renown French poet, deacon, schoolmaster and archdeacon of the ninth century stated that malachite should be worn as a talisman for young people to protect them from evil and aid in sleep. Throughout history this stone has been used for protection by numerous peoples and would often be engraved with a figure of the sun to protect from a wide range of dangers including lightning strikes and disease. During the Middle Ages malachite was often worn by Capricorns to avert depression, which they were believed to be especially vulnerable to. Evil eye talismans are commonly made from malachite due to these warding capabilities.

Malachite is first and foremost a stone of protection, it absorbs pollutants and negative energies from your body and your environment. It can guard against the negative effects of radiation and electromagnetic pollution and restores and grounds the spirit with its strong earth energies. Malachite can help prevent fatigue associated with being around electronic equipment and fluorescent lighting. The properties of this stone also help with the dangers associated with travel, especially the fears and anxieties that come with it.

Malachite is a diuretic stone and can help with kidney and gallstones, it may also help with issues arising from osteoarthritis and strengthen cognition and memory as we age. Malachite energy aligns and resonates with the heart chakra and can purify the physical body, aiding in all matters associated with circulatory health.

Moldavite

The Extraterrestrial Stone of Connection

Moldavite is a vitreous silica tektite glass that was formed by a meteorite impact in southern Germany over 14 million years ago. Moldavite ranges in color from forest green to a blue-greenish color with varying degrees of translucence. The name moldavite comes from the name of the Moldau river in the Czech Republic where the first described pieces were found. Moldavite was formed when an asteroid collided with the site now known as the Nördlinger Ries Crater, materials from the impact were melted upon collision and thrown into the air where they cooled before falling across central and eastern Europe.

Moldavite is a stone of connectivity that carries an intense earthly frequency, the origins of this stone lend to it being known as a fiery stone of passion and action. Simply holding this stone creates a sense of warmness throughout the body, coupled with a sense of kinetic drive and action. Moldavite has been used for practical and spiritual purposes since the stone age, used for myriad purposes such as arrowheads, cutting tools, and has even been found at the religious site of Venus of Willendorf, the oldest known goddess statue. According to Czech lore this stone was frequently gifted at betrothal ceremonies to promote harmony and healthy marital relations and is known to be a powerful stone of spiritual transformation.

Moldavite, with its radiant green energy, is mostly associated with the heart but with its extremely high vibrational energies can activate all of the chakra centers. When the Heart Chakra is out of balance it can cause feelings of imbalance in relationships, meditating with this stone can promote feelings of equality and meaning in our interactions with others. Given the cosmic origin of this stone it has the innate ability to connect our consciousness with the Universal Source, leading to new discoveries about our selves and the greater meaning in the universe. Moldavite can help us understand harmony and balance within a world seemingly dictated by chaos, this is especially helpful to those struggling with anxiety and issues with uncertainty.

Moonstone

The Travelers Stone

Moonstone is a sodium potassium aluminum silicate type of feldspar. It can come in a variety of colors including grey, blue, pink, peach, green and brown with white being the most common. Moonstone has been used for thousands of years as a stone of protection for travelers and is said to be especially useful while traveling at night. Moonstone is a common wedding gift in India where it is said to bring harmony to the relationship. The Romans believed that moonstone was created by solidified light from the moon, both the Romans and the Greeks associated it with their lunar deities.

Moonstones are first and foremost a stone of travelers due to the protection it provides those traveling at night, it would often be used on ships and by traveling merchants who would frequently find themselves traversing dark and perilous roads and waterways plagued by bandits, pirates, and wild animals. Moonstone can be carried with you while out and about to ensure safe travels, consider putting this stone in the glovebox of your vehicle to help ward negative energies and outcomes.

Moonstone is also a stone of fertility, its divine feminine energy can stimulate the kundalini and charge the libido. Use moonstone to encourage pregnancy and to reignite the passionate energies of a relationship that has dulled with time. Wear a moonstone necklace during lovemaking to align one's energies with the Lunar cycle. Moonstone in general can help us realign to the natural cycles of the world, putting us back into harmony and reducing feelings of apprehension, anxiety, and depression. Use this stone to help connect with the divine feminine and while communing with the goddess. Moonstone is extremely effective in regard to feminine affirmation, especially in those that are experiencing dysphoria.

Moonstones are associated with the Crown Chakra and can promote oneness with the goddess through our spiritual center. The crown chakra is the source of our spirituality and cosmic identity, using moonstone with this chakra point in mind can lead to broadened self-discovery and the knowledge to help develop feminine clairvoyance and strength.

Obsidian

The Mirror Stone of Truth

Obsidian is a type of igneous rock that forms when lava from a volcano rapidly cools with minimal crystal growth. Lava that is rich in oxygen, aluminium, sodium, potassium, and silicon is cooled quickly and the high viscosity caused by the high silica content cause the lava to form into a highly reflective, natural volcanic glass. Obsidian has been used since prehistoric time to craft weaponry and tools due to the sharp edges that occur upon fracturing and has been prized throughout antiquity for its beauty and reflective properties.

Work with obsidian to reveal hidden truths, especially in terms of the self. Those who dare to gaze into an obsidian reflection will be made witness to the entirety of their beings. Obsidian is a stone of truth and the visions it induces can be helpful in finding one's inner truth by cutting through all the negative emotions that cloud our ability to perceive ourselves as we truly are. Obsidian is also believed to be able to show us truths outside of ourselves and can be used as a sort of looking glass to see the world as it is. These clairvoyant and revealing properties are excellent when uncertainty and apprehension prevent us from being able to make clear headed decisions, sometimes we want to believe things are the way we prefer them to be and not how they actually are, obsidian can help cut through our biases. Obsidian can be especially useful to people in professions that deal with people that might not be forthcoming with the information you need to help them, including but not limited to doctors, nurses, psychiatrists, and teachers.

Obsidian is an extremely powerful grounding stone that resonates with the root chakra, it creates a tether from the root chakra to the earth aiding in the stability of our emotions and actions while stimulating growth. Use this stone during meditation to detach from the conscience mind when you want to do some heavy soul searching and self-realization, you'll stay tethered to the spirit while your mind explores the deepest recesses of your soul leading to unmatched understanding and actualization.

Onyx

The Stone of Courage

Onyx is a parallel banded type of chalcedony, which is a cryptocrystalline form of silica. The name onyx comes from the Latin/Greek word "Onyx" which means "claw". While black is the most common color for onyx it can also be red (known as sardonyx) and green/yellow in color. It's common for onyx to be treated with different chemicals, a technique that has been practiced for thousands of years, to bring out the contrast in the bands that give onyx is unique look and is said to not effect the stones natural powers.

Onyx has been used for thousands of years to carve everything from talismans that warriors would wear to instill courage, usually with the God of War Mars carved into the stone, to dishware and jewelry. Women would place a piece of sardonyx between their breast during childbirth to grant confidence and aid in the delivery. The Persians believed that Onyx could help in the treatment of epilepsy and would carve amulets to be worn to prevent seizures. Onyx has also been used as a scrying stone for thousands of years and is considered to be one of the best stones for this purpose and it's still commonly made into pendulums today.

 It should be noted that some cultures, especially in Asia considered black onyx to be a stone of misfortune with the potential to cause bad dreams, depression, and loss of energy although the sources of these claims seem to be inconsistent and seem to be more of an indicator that the stone has a dual nature. It's said that sardonyx (red onyx) would often be used in tandem with black onyx to negate the negative influence of the latter.

Onyx can be used as a protector stone due to its ability to instill courage and strengthen resolve, giving us the drive to accomplish things that we'd otherwise doubt ourselves to the point of failure. It should be kept in mind that too much courage can be a bad thing and potentially lead to misfortune which is likely why onyx gets a bad reputation in some cultures, not every mountain needs to be climbed, through meditation we can come to understand the difference between can and should. That being said onyx can be a wonderful stone for those who lack self-respect and determination, strengthening intuition and giving us insight to our own hidden abilities.

Onyx stimulates the base chakra and can help us stay connected to the earth energies needed to ground us and keep our energies regulated and flowing smoothly, the white bands of the onyx stone stimulate the crown chakra, aligning these two chakras can be very beneficial to exploring cosmic realities while staying firmly grounded to reality.

Opal

The Vision Stone

Opal is a hydrated amorphous type of silica with a water content that can range anywhere between 3 and 21% and can occur within the fissures of almost any type of rock. The name opal is thought to be derived from the Sanskrit word "upala" meaning "jewel" and the Greek "opállios" meaning "to see a change in color" as opals presents in a wide variety of colors. In antiquity opal was a very rare and prized gem that was a favorite of kings and queens across Europe as it could only be found in one location in Cervenica which was beyond the boundaries of Ancient Rome. New mines have been located since the 19th century, notably in Australia which today produces approximately 95% of worlds opal supply.

An old Hindu legend tells the story of the Mother Goddess creating the first Opal, she transformed the Virgin Goddess into an opal to hide her from her suitors, this has led to opal being known as a stone of concealment. Opal can be used in situations where you'd like to fly under the radar and keep attention off you. Being the center of attention can be draining and this stone can help prevent unwanted advances from those who wish to disrupt our tranquility.

Opal is also a stone of healing and can be especially beneficial in terms of eye, nails, hair and skin health. Opal is believed to be capable of dispersing infections and purifying the blood and kidneys by utilizing the body's natural ability to wash out impurities. Opal is also known as a water stone due to its high water content giving it the ability to help with the regulation of water levels in the body, aiding in preventing dehydration and bloating due to water buildup in the body. Opal can also be used to purify our emotional states, bringing blocked and repressed thoughts and feelings to the surface so we may deal with them accordingly.

Opals multi-colored nature and frequency range make it useful in activating all the chakra points, linking them to the Crown Chakra to stimulate healing and emotional growth. Opal can be very overwhelming to use during meditation but over time you will become accustomed to this fiery energetic stone and learn to harmonize with its transformative and cleansing powers.

Peridot

The Gem of Extreme Transformation

Peridot, also known as chrysolite, is a magnesium-rich type of olivine silicate that gets its green color from the iron content within the gem. The origin of the name peridot is unknown, although its thought to be an alteration of the anglo-norman word "pedoretés" which is a kind of opal. Peridots translucent green coloring leads it to often be mistaken for emerald as they share many characteristics.

Peridot has been long prized for its rarity and its ability to prevent nightmares and stifle fear, known as the "extreme gem" due to the fact that this gem isn't formed in the Earths crust like most gems but like diamonds in the molten rock of the upper mantle, only brought to the surface due to extreme events such as earthquakes and volcanos. This stone, forged in fire, is a powerful protector for dark magics and sorceries and has been worn for millennia to protect from these malignant forces. The nature and origins of this stone lend to its transformative powers, when change is needed this stone can provide, it's especially useful for those trying to overcome addiction or lethargy. These properties also make it useful in helping positive change occur in relationships, giving us the courage and power to demand change or end it all together.

Peridot activates the Heart Chakra, it can aid in regulating our interactions with the world around us, clearing the fog that can set in with overwhelming situations, helping us maintain our identities and project truth and reason in tumultuous situations. Meditation with peridot can aid in self-realization and help us better understand our emotions and how our actions affect those around us, it can help us with all matters of the heart and can give us an introspective view on what we think we feel and what we actually feel, clarifying any doubts and solidifying what we know to be right. Peridots transformative properties can also be used with meditation to improve things that we deem to be negative qualities, it can allow us to objectively examine our emotions of greed, envy, malice, fear and jealousy and transform them into qualities that we prefer such as self-acceptance, gratitude, compassion, and acceptance.

Pyrite

Pyrite is a mineral composed of iron and sulfur and is the most abundant sulfide mineral. The metallic luster of pyrite has led to it being referred to as "fools gold" or "brass/brazzle". While pyrite might not share the same rarity and prestige as gold, it certainly has many practical and metaphysical uses. Pyrite has been mentioned in writings dating back to Ancient Rome and was written about by Pliny the Elder who mentioned its brassy luster and its ability to create sparks when struck against steel. These qualities led to pyrite being used in early firearms and it's still used by some indigenous peoples for its ability to start fires today. It still has many industrial uses, remaining one of the primary methods of obtaining sulfur dioxide and is an integral material in the production of lithium batteries. The name pyrite comes from the Greek word "pyr" meaning "fire".

Pyrite was used as a protective stone by Native Americans, specifically the Americans of Mesoamerica. Pyrite would be polished to create mirrors that could reflect evil spirits and energies and would often be placed in burial sites to ensure the deceased were able to rest in peace. Pyrite can be used for similar purposes today, acting as a ward that prevents any negative energies from invading your person or place. Pyrite can be placed in the home, workplace, or in your car to protect you from the negative outcomes brought about by toxic energies that run rampant in today's world. Pyrite is also said to stimulate blood flow, encouraging mental clarity, recall, and focus. Pyrite emits radiant masculine energy and can help with feelings of subservience, ineptitude and inferiority, helping us escape from situations where we feel trapped and dominated, encouraging a strong emotional state that can lead us to be more self-reliant and confident in our choices and actions.

Pyrite stimulates the Solar Plexus Chakra which governs energy distribution and relationships, developing this Chakra can lead to better immune health and higher levels of energy due to an increased level of oxygenated blood flow. Meditating with pyrite can help us come to realizations that make us better partners in business and relationships, giving us the confidence we need to not be taken advantage of and the nerve to take charge of a situation where we otherwise might be crippled by self-doubt.

Quartz

The Universal Stone

Quartz is a crystalline silicon dioxide mineral, its atoms are linked in a continuous tetrahedral framework lending to its impressive shape, beauty and energies. Quartz is the second most abundant mineral on the Earth's crust with only feldspar being more common. Quartz comes in a variety of colors and has been prized for millennia for its brilliance and has been an integral part of commerce and culture, spiritual and scientific. Quartz ritual items and jewelry have been found the world over and have been an important part of numerous spiritual practices and has played an enormous role in the evolution of our species. Quartz has too many practical applications to list but here are a few to give you an idea of how important this crystal has been to the development of technology: watches, ultrasound equipment, microphones, radio tech, memory chips, and electronic circuitry. The reason quartz is so useful is due to its pyroelectric and piezoelectric properties, which give it the ability to transform heat and mechanical pressure into electromagnetic energy, the importance and power of this stone can't be overstated.

When the lay-person thinks of crystals they're generally thinking of this stone, it's six-sided prisms that radiate light in all the colors of the rainbow have become ingrained in the minds of even the most mundane of people not only due to the beauty of quartz, but many have become aware of the power this crystal holds. Truly a gift from mother earth for all of its children, this abundant gem has unmatched powers of healing and cleansing and its quite common to see a person in possession of one of these crystals even if they aren't an expert in the field of metaphysics and crystal science.

The same properties that make quartz so useful in the technological world make it one of the best stones for spiritual growth and transformation, this stone has the power to transmute our negative attributes and energies into more positive and desirable traits. This ability can also be used to not only transmute but amplify the energies of other crystals when used in tandem. When used in ritual work it can not only act as a purifying element, restricting the influence of negative disruptive energies but can also amplify the effects of the rituals. Quartz can also open up pathways when trying to connect with the spirit world and is exceptionally useful when communing with and honoring our ancestors and deities.

Quartz is also a stone of intellect, bringing clarity and dispelling doubt in our abilities. It can encourage brain health and can cleanse our minds of negative damaging energies that plague our psyches causing frustration, anxiety and depression. These purifying qualities can also cleanse the rest of our bodies, expunging toxins and harmful energies that build up in our circulatory systems, organs, and muscles but is exceptionally great at healing the nervous system.

It should be apparent by now that quartz is particularly active with the Crown Chakra, bringing enlightenment, clarity, and connection with the divine, but quartz, with its plethora of prismatic energy, has the capacity to stimulate all 7 Chakras. Use quartz to bring about absolute harmony to all the chakral regions, balancing your body and its systems to an optimal level. Quartz is frequently touted as one of the most important crystals to have and use and it's easy to see why, its uses are near endless and its powers unmatched, if you only have one crystal this is the one to have.

Rhodolite

Stone of Emotional Healing and Inspiration

Rhodolite is the name used for the red to rose-pink pyrope silicate which is a variety of garnet. Rhodolite's color is determined by the amount of iron, chromium, manganese and vanadium found within the stone. The name rhodolite comes from the Greek word "rhodon" which means "rose-like".

Rhodolite is a stone of inspiration, connecting us to our spiritual guides that lead us to new frontiers of creativity and universal understanding. It helps us navigate our spiritual path while helping us to understand the things we experience along the way. A favorite stone of artists, writers and creators of all kinds, gazing into this wondrous stone can spark a creative attitude and mindset in the most downtrodden and defeated of people.

These properties make this stone one of the best for healing from emotional trauma and the aura poisoning effects that come along with it. Abuse of any kind leaves a mark on our souls that must be overcame, which isn't always easy. Rhodolite can help us overcome feelings of guilt and self-blame that prevent us from seeing the truth of a traumatic event, we often get stuck thinking about how we could have done things differently to produce a better outcome and we neglect the fact that sometimes things are out of our control. Rhodolite helps us set aside those destructive feelings and emotions of past contemplation and lets us look towards the future, coming out stronger and more resilient than ever.

In regard to chakra work, rhodolite resonates strongly with the heart chakra, healing, restoring, and developing positive outlooks to help you achieve positive outcomes, no matter how much damage has been done to the region. Rhodolite connects the Heart Chakra to the Root and the Crown, allowing a restoration of the balances needed for clarity and truthful thinking. We often misplace the blame for trauma onto ourselves, when our Base, Heart, and Crown are working in unison we can see things for how they really are, placing the blame on the aggressor and working towards building ourselves back stronger than ever.

Rose Quartz
The Heart Stone

Rose quartz is a type of quartz that contains trace amounts of iron, manganese, or titanium, giving it a pink to reddish hue. Rose quartz is also known as "hyaline quartz, which comes from the Greek word "hyalos" meaning "glass" and was known in ancient times as "bohemian ruby".

Rose quartz is often referred to as "The Heart Stone" due to its strong relation to the Heart Chakra, it's a stone of love and nurturing. Rose quartz can be used in all manner of rituals pertaining to relationships, to strengthen and repair bonds between lovers and family members. This stone is especially helpful to new mothers that are trying to navigate the often confusing and overwhelming job they have taken upon themselves. Rose quartz can bring out the innate ability that all mothers have to care for and nurture their child, granting patience, understanding and the calm demeanor needed to raise a child in today's world while calming anxieties and fears one might have as a new mother. Pregnant mothers can meditate with this stone near the stomach to help strengthen the bond between them and their unborn child, it can also promote healthy development, especially in regard to heart and circulatory health. Carry this stone with you to the delivery room to help ensure a healthy and smooth delivery.

Rose quartz status as a "love stone" means it can be used for a variety of reasons regarding relationships. Rose quartz can be especially useful in rituals done to promote self-love and growth, it can also be used to help you find love and friendship by meditating with rose quartz while concentrating on feelings of companionship and envisioning what you want from the relationship you seek.

Rose quartz is the stone most associated with the Heart Chakra, and for good reason, this stone has an unmatched ability to open up the heart chakra, allowing us to give and be more receptive of love. This stone can purify the body and the spirit of toxic impurities that block our ability to regulate our emotions, aiding us in self growth and maturation. This stone of the Mother Goddess links our hearts to the earth, grounding our emotions, making us more empathetic and caring while aiding in the elimination of fear, hatred, and resentment.

Ruby

The King of Gems

Rubies are a variety of the mineral corundum, other varieties of corundum are called sapphires. Ruby gets its vibrant red color from the replacement of a small percentage of aluminium atoms of a normal corundum with chromium atoms. Rubies are the third hardest gemstone only being outclassed by moissanite and the hardest of gems, diamond. Ruby is considered one of the "four precious gemstones" alongside Diamond, Sapphire, and Emerald.

Rubies have long been prized around the world as a signifier of wealth, power, and prominence. This is led to it being known as "The King of Gems" and it has been used for thousands of years to adorn the crowns, armor, and weaponry of countless royal families. Legends regarding the power of rubies pervade nearly every ancient culture and it was commonly held higher in value than even that of diamonds, so valuable that the great emperor Kublai Khan was said to have exchanged an entire city for a single large ruby. Examples of ancient usage are widespread, especially in Asian regions. Hindus believe rubies to be the "gemstone of the sun" and can bring favor from the heavenly deity Surya, leader of the nine heavenly bodies. Ancient peoples that had the resources to get access to rubies would use them in a plethora of ways, most notably as a stone of fortune and protection often being sewn into clothing or included in the construction of a new property, it was even said that a ruby surgically inserted into the body had the ability to grant complete invulnerability to the wielder.

Ruby is a "blood stone" like several other red gems, in that it promotes hearth health and circulation, it's a gem of passion and its fiery energies can be a powerful aphrodisiac due to these properties. Rubies can also promote wealth and fortune and put us in the right mindset to achieve our dreams and goals by granting courage in the face of adversities and challenges, they can sharpen our wits and make us more aware of things that might otherwise escape our notice, all of these qualities lend to the idea that usage of this stone can lead to prosperity as our ancestors believed.

Ruby vibrates at the frequency of the Base Chakra and can stimulate our life-force energy, also known as chi. The Base Chakra, also known as the Root Chakra, located at the base of the spine, governs all things in our bodies related to energy and energy distribution. When this chakra is unaligned and unbalanced it can cause feelings of lethargy, depression, and a defeatist attitude that leads us to failure and isolation. Meditate with this stone near the Base Chakra to connect to the earth's energies, revitalizing and reinvigorating your own stores of energies that ruby can help regulate and properly distribute.

Sapphire
The Stone of Wisdom

Sapphire is a variety of the mineral corundum that consists of aluminium oxide with other trace elements such as chromium, titanium, iron, vanadium, or magnesium. The name sapphire comes from the Greek "sapheiros" and Latin "saphirus" meaning "blue". Sapphires are generally blue but can come in other colors such as purple, orange, green and yellow, these are known as "fancy sapphires" and when corundum presents as red due to inclusions of chromium it is known as a ruby. When two or more colors present in a corundum it is known as a "parti sapphire".

Sapphires, much like rubies, have a wide range of applications in the industrial world, used to make everything from watches to complicated lasers and computer parts. Sapphires have long been revered for their rarity and lustrous beauty, known as one of the 4 "precious gemstones". Sapphires have been worn and used in talismans by many notable historical figures, Hebrew legend states that Abraham and King Solomon both possessed talismans of Sapphire and it's said that the law passed down to

Moses on Mount Sinai were engraved upon tablets of sapphire. The Ancient Greeks of Delphi would wear a sapphire when seeking wisdom from the Oracle at Apollo's shrine, Hindus believed sapphire to be the stone of Shani (Saturn) and would great the wearer the favor of the gods and Buddhists believed the stone would bring spiritual enlightenment and devotion. Many kings passed down rings of sapphire, which was said to promote insight and wisdom.

Sapphire is first and foremost a stone of wisdom and understanding and can be a great crystal for anyone in an academic field or anyone wishing to broaden their understanding of any topic, be it scholastic or metaphysical. Sapphire helps us take in information and see it in an outside the box way, allowing us to critically analyze the things we learn and experience with a degree of separation from our selves.

Sapphire stimulates the Third Eye and Throat Chakras, allowing us to perceive things as they are, take them in and understand them and then relay that information to others, shaping thought into form. It grants us discipline and helps us adhere to the order that we've created to accomplish our goals and stay on our spiritual paths. Meditating with sapphire can help strengthen our resolve, understand difficult things and work through our problems, it's also a very effective influencer of dreams and can help with nightmares and restlessness that lead us to experience exhaustion and clouded thoughts.

Selenite

Stone of The Moon Goddess

Selenite is a type of gypsum and is composed of calcium sulfate dihydrate, selenite crystals are some of the largest crystals that are found in the world with the largest being 12 meters long and weighing over 55 tons. It is one of the softest crystals and can be scratched with just a fingernail. Selenite has a pearly luster and is transparent and colorless, any colors or opacity that occur in the crystal is due to the presence of other minerals. Selenite is the most common sulfate mineral and is found all over the world.

Selenite gets its name from the Greek "selēnē" meaning "moon", as the stone is closely associated with the waxing and waning cycles of the moon in relation to the Goddess of the Moon, Selene. This stone is often used to represent the moon goddess and it radiates feminine energy, encouraging harmony, fidelity, fertility, and motherly love. Selenite can be used to create an orderly environment that is catered to spiritual growth and enlightenment and is a common inclusion on ritual altars for its representational and energetic properties. Selenite encourages peace and understanding between family members and coworkers, it can aid in judgement and insight leading to positive resolutions to during negotiations or disagreements.

Selenite resonates with the Crown Chakra and acts as a gateway to the Universal Self, it can help us take control of our thoughts and actions and connect us to higher planes of being and consciousness. Selenite acts as a doorway to higher states of being and through meditation and can lead us to a better understanding of ourselves and the universe while promoting peace and acceptance of those truths. Selenite can help us connect with our spirit/angel guides and ancestors who will help us grow and understand things that we have yet to grasp, giving us insight into the past and future while granting us the wisdom to understand those revelations as they are and not how we wish them to be.

Sodalite

Stone of Logic and Reason

Sodalite is a tectosilicate mineral that consists mostly of sodium from which it gets its name. Sodalite is a hard yet fragile mineral that is generally a royal blue color with white streaks although sodalite can also be grey, yellow, pink, or green which are much more uncommon.

Sodalites tranquil energies spark thought and critical thinking, a stone of rational thinking and logic it can dispel neurotic thought patterns and irrational anxieties. An excellent stone for deep meditative sessions, sodalite can be used to enter a state of peaceful introspection that allows us to think clearly about ourselves and formulate consistent thought patterns that can help alleviate anxiety, depression, and self-esteem problems.

Sodalite is great at aiding us in problem solving of all types, it allows us to think practically and tackle any situation that might present itself and can promote unity in group projects that involve collective effort and cooperation and can be a great stone to have for anyone in a profession that involves lots of mental clarity and on the spot problem solving. Sodalite is a calming crystal full of peaceful tranquil energy so it can also be used as a sleep aid by placing it underneath your pillow to eliminate any chaotic thought patterns that prevent you from falling and staying asleep.

The blue energy of Sodalite stimulates the Throat Chakra, when this Chakra is blocked or out of balance it can affect our ability to express our thoughts and emotions, the Throat Chakra is a sort of pressure valve from which all the energies from the lower chakras are expressed and released. Sodalite can also activate the Brow Chakra which is where it gets its reputation as a stone of logic and reason, with this chakra activated we can see things as they are and interpret them in a logical way that is free from the emotions that may cloud our ability to see and process information in an objective way.

Sunstone

The Fiery Stone of Leadership

Sunstone is a mineral within the feldspar family, the optical effect of sunstone is caused by reflections from the inclusion of minute copper scales within the stone causing a schiller effect. The copper inclusions give sunstone a similar appearance to aventurine which has led to sunstone also being referred to as aventurine-feldspar. Sunstone generally has an orangish hue but can also come in hues of green and blue but can also be completely colorless.

A stone of fire and warmth, sunstone evokes innate leadership qualities in all that utilize it. The energy that radiates from this breath-taking stone can bring out our inner-power and grant confidence and personal power. Sunstone reinvigorates passion, promoting action and determination by igniting the flame within our spirit. It is also a stone of abundance and prosperity, guiding us to take the necessary steps to gain independence from the things in life which tether us to mediocrity, helping us accomplish self-reliance, materially and emotionally. Sunstone also helps with conquering our phobias and can give us the courage needed to face the most daunting of tasks that we'd normally let self-doubt and fear prevent us from doing.

Sunstone activates the Base and Sacral Chakras, energizing these areas stimulating will, leadership qualities, and sexuality. Focusing on these chakras can help us understand what we want from life, from our professions, our partners, and our friends, and can give us the strength and grounding to go get it. When these chakras are out of balance we can fall into patterns of dependence and self-pity, brought by a mindset that isn't grounded and lacks understanding of our power. This stone works amazingly with moonstone, the yin to this stone's yang, allowing us to achieve perfect balance and harmony that comes from the coalescence of the god and goddess.

Tanzanite

The Stone of Transmutation

Tanzanite is a variety of the mineral zoisite, the blues and purples that differentiate this stone from other zoisites is caused by small amounts of vanadium inside the stone, this stone is also known as Blue Zoisite. Tanzanite is one of the rarest gemstones in the world and is rarer than diamonds, being found in one location in Africa, The Republic of Tanzania.

Tanzanite is a stone of spiritual transmutation that can aid us in the exploration of psychic being. With its high vibrational energies, tanzanite has the ability to safely connect us to the higher realms, allowing us to retain our conscience selves while maintaining our ability to stay grounded while journeying into the deepest recesses of the spirit. If you can manage to acquire a tanzanite stone, given its high value and rarity, it's one of the best stones for the development of psychic powers and activating the third eye, keep in mind that even the smallest of tanzanite stones can be extremely powerful and effective. When worn as jewelry tanzanite has the power to lift us up to a higher plane of consciousness with effects that radiate to everyone around us, granting insight and understanding of the mundane world and how it is inseparable from the spirit.

Tanzanite stimulates the crown, third eye, and throat chakras, granting us both the understanding that comes from higher states of being and the ability to communicate that understanding to others. It also has the power to connect the Third Eye and Heart Chakras, which is why this stone is so good at spirit transmutation, giving us the ability to look into our souls and perceive the spirit world as it actually is, granting us the introspective knowledge needed to elevate ourselves to higher planes of being.

Tiger's Eye

The Stone of Divine Sight

Tiger's Eye is a gemstone in the quartz family, it gets its lustrous, silky appearance from the parallel intergrowth of amphibole fibers and quartz crystals creating an effect known as chatoyance. Tiger's Eye has been prized for thousands of years, dating all the way back to the Egyptians who would facet the stones onto statues of their gods and goddesses, this stone represented both the Sun God Ra and the God of the Earth Geb and granted divine sight. In the East this stone was representative of the Tiger Spirit, King of beasts, and promoted strength, valor, peace, and harmony. Romans would wear Tigers eye stones into battle, with the belief that it could protect them from harm and even deflect oncoming attacks.

Tiger's Eye is a stone of sight and can be beneficial to all things related to eye health. This stones role as a vision stone isn't only limited to physical eye health, but spiritual as well. Use this stone to develop one's intuition and abilities of perception, developing these skills can allow us to see through trickery and manipulation, granting the wisdom to observe the world in a way in which we can see all the innerworkings and mechanisms that contribute to the universal whole. Tiger's Eye can help us critically analyze ourselves and honestly see the flaws that are holding us back, giving us the courage to meet these flaws with valor and forge a new outlook and attitude. It can help us overcome things such as addiction and dependency, allowing us to not only see the problem but to also see the solutions and the steps we need to take to improve our conditions.

Tiger's Eye stimulates the Solar Plexus, Sacral, and Root Chakras. These chakras are extremely important to maintaining order and balance within our bodies, connecting the Sacral Chakra with the Root Chakra allowing us to be passionate and strong-willed while maintaining firm grounding. These energies are then distributed through the Solar Plexus which promotes health and spiritual balance throughout the entire body, when the Solar Plexus chakra isn't aligned and functioning as it should we can become overwhelmed by feelings of apprehension and fear of disappointment, allowing our lives and will to be dictated by others who might not have our best interests at heart. Meditate with this stone near the naval while focusing on the powers of Earth and Fire within this stone to develop these chakras to harness the power of this stone and take charge of your life with dignity and fiery resilience.

Topaz

The Stone of Focus and Clarity

Topaz is a nesosilicate mineral of fluorine and aluminum. On its own topaz is colorless but often presents in brown, pale blue, and yellow orange depending on the trace amounts of impurities such as chromium within the stone. Topaz can also be heat treated to make it deep blue, pale green, reddish-orange, purple, or pink. The most common variety and the one that typically comes to mind when thinking of topaz is the brownish/golden yellow variety.

Prior to modern times the name topaz was used to refer to any yellowish stone, including the less rare citrine and peridot. The ancient Romans believed that topaz stones could protect travelers from harm, during the Middle Ages people would attach a topaz stone to their left arm to protect from the evil eye and curses. The English believed that topaz had the ability to cure a variety of mental illnesses and would use it to treat what they referred to as "lunacy", in India the stone was used to ensure long life, beauty and intelligence.

Topaz is a stone of the sun and sky and has the power to magnify our innate abilities by intensifying our focus and intention. Any energies that are directed through topaz are multiplied many times over and enhanced, our manifestations made clear with a laser focus that helps ensure the success of our efforts. Topaz can help with clarity of thought and can be a great addition to any ritual practice or daily affirmation work. Visualization, meditation and projection are all enhanced by this stone as it aids in the connection to the realm of the divine, clarifying our intentions by blocking out distracting thoughts that hamper our manifestation efforts and block communication with the universal spirit. Focus and intention are the most important elements of manifestation and mental blockages can prevent us from fully realizing our abilities to manifest, this clarifying stone can help us break the mental fog that prevents us from achieving our goals.

Topaz's qualities of clarification can be helpful in a wide range of ways, it can be used to uncover lies, see through manipulation and bring hidden truths to light. Topaz is known for its ability to bring forth true love, likely due to is power of revelation, allowing us to see through the facades of those who only wish to use us in selfish ways. Topaz is also known to bring good fortune though its ability to help us achieve our goals by helping maintain a healthy mind state regardless of stressful circumstances and contributing to our overall well-being.

Topaz can activate different chakras depending on the color, blue topaz is associated with the Brow and Throat Chakras and has the ability to free us from negative emotions and unwanted thoughts. Blockage of this chakra can lead to self-doubt and anxieties that keep us from speaking our truths and engaging in constructive ways. Golden shades of topaz are ideal for working on the development of the Solar Plexus Chakra and the elimination of fears that keep us from reaching our full potential. Meditate with this stone while focusing on the alleviation of these negative emotions to encourage faith in ourselves and nurture the optimism needed to manifest our dreams and desires.

Tourmaline

Tourmaline is a crystalline boron silicate mineral that is compounded with elements such as iron, magnesium, aluminium, sodium, potassium, or lithium. Tourmaline can be a variety of colors, but a vast majority of tourmaline is of the black variety, also known as schorl, which is thought to make up around 95% of all tourmalines found in nature. The name tourmaline comes from the Sinhalese word "tōramalli", which refers to carnelian gemstones which are varieties of the silica mineral chalcedony.

Tourmaline has been an interesting and useful stone to many chemists for hundreds of years due to its pyroelectric properties, which means that they are naturally electronically polarized creating a large electric field that can produce an electric current through heating or cooling of the stone. This fascinating attribute of tourmaline has led to it being known as the "Ceylonese Sri Lankan Magnet" due to its ability to attract and repel hot ashes from a campfire.

These unique properties have led Tourmaline to be used by magicians throughout antiquity to protect and shield them from evil spirits as they conducted their magic and is often used in the same way today. A powerful protector stone that can dispel negative energies and other destructive forces. It has the ability to draw out negative energies from our auras and ground them, neutralizing their caustic influences to maintain positive vibes and feelings of tranquility. Tourmaline also repels the harmful effects of radiation, light, and electrical pollutants. These powers of repulsion are due to the field that is naturally created by the physical composition of this miraculous stone.

Use this stone in your home to bring protection and shielding from all the disruptive energetic bombardment that is invisible to the eye but effects our spirits and aura due to modern technology and the toxic vibration emanated by modern hustle and bustle mentality. This stone is also great for any high stress workplace, giving you a bubble of protection to help you focus and maintain your auric equilibrium amongst the chaos. Tourmaline is a great stone to use in terms of ritual practice as well, ensuring that your intention and focus is not disrupted and derailed by outside energies that can interfere with proper manifestation.

Black Tourmaline is extremely effective in activating grounding between the Root Chakra and Earth Energies. The Root Chakra is the foundation of spiritual and physical energies in the body, when this chakra isn't grounded, it can lead to lethargy, depression, and lack of enthusiasm for things you'd normally be passionate about. Blockage in the Root Chakra can create detachment from reality and an inability for the other chakras to function properly. Meditation with tourmaline can ground the root chakra, leading to the revitalization of our stores of energy which is needed to ensure our auras are operating at optimal frequencies, giving us the attitude and motivation we need to seize the day with clarity and confidence.

Turquoise

The Universal Stone

Turquoise is a hydrated phosphate of aluminium and copper with a triclinic crystal system. Turquoise is opaque and is blueish green in color with Tibetan Turquoise being more green in nature. One of the oldest recorded stones to exist, beads dating back 7,000 years have been found in modern day Iraq and Egyptian turquoise mines have been found dating back to 3,200 B.C., many Egyptian and American burial items, such as masks, were inlaid with this stone and the Aztecs would carve many grave-items such as ornate inlaid skulls that have sparked interest and curiosity to this day.

Cultures from all around the world, from nearly every time period treasured turquoise. Native Americans also used turquoise to adorn their burial sites for protection and the stone would be worn for ceremonial reasons to represent the Spirit of the Sky. Turquoise has come to be known as The Universal Stone due to its widespread usage and its ability to connect us with the Universal Spirit which has led it to be utilized by many peoples for burial rights as it bridges the gap between material plane and the spiritual.

Turquoise reinforces the energy fields of the body, enhancing our ability to communicate with the spiritual world. It can promote intuition and help during deep meditation, opening up channels to higher planes. It is a stone of wholeness, ensuring safety during travels and helping us hold on to the things that we cherish, whether they be physical or emotional. It unites the earth and sky, creating a link between the female and male energies that are needed for true harmonic balance. Turquoise allows us to examine all the parts of ourselves, our positive attributes and our flaws and how they work together to make us who we are, this is especially useful when critically analyzing ourselves and can help us realize what flaws should be worked on and which ones are actually useful and contribute to our overall well-being.

Turquoise stimulates the Throat Chakra, enabling us to project our inner wisdom in a way that's understood and fosters connections with others while decreasing the likelihood of alienation or feelings of condescension. The clearing and empowering of this chakra can help us overcome feelings of shyness and embarrassment that come with public speaking and can embolden us to speak our mind when we take issue with something being done or said that affect us or the ones we wish to protect.

Cleansing

Crystals have memories, they absorb the energies and react to the people and places around them, that energy builds up over time and it's recommended to do regular cleansing rituals. These rituals can be done monthly or on a weekly basis if they're getting a lot of usage. It's also a good idea to cleanse any new crystals that you might acquire, be they purchased or gifted.

There are many different ways to cleanse crystals and some methods are better than others depending on the stone you are cleansing. I'm going to go over a few of my favorite methods and detail which stones should or shouldn't be used with said methods.

Sunlight

Sunlight is one of the most popular ways to cleanse a crystal, the radiant yang energy of the sun brings balance to the yin earth energy of your crystals. Just place your crystals in a sunny window seal for a few minutes and the suns purifying rays will cleanse your crystals. Rose quartz, amber, and amethyst can potentially fade from direct exposure to sunlight so if using this method to cleanse them place them in indirect sunlight at dawn to prevent discoloration.

Moonlight

Moonlight is a great alternative to sunlight as the energies from the moon are much more delicate and prevents the risk of discoloration. The full moon is the ideal time to do this kind of cleansing and can be a great way to start tracking moon cycles while giving you a monthly ritual to perform that will bring you closer and familiarize you to the waxing and waning cycles that is perfectly represented in the changing visage of the moon. As this form of cleansing uses much gentler energies I suggest leaving your crystals to cleanse for a few hours as opposed to the minutes that direct sunlight requires.

Other Crystals

Some crystals are self-cleansing and don't hold onto energy in the same manner as other crystals. Crystals such as amethyst, quartz, selenite, tourmaline, and carnelian negate the energies they take in and can be used to cleanse other crystals. Simply place one of these stones in a jar or other vessel and let them sit for 24 hours to fully cleanse your crystals. This method is especially useful for delicate crystals that can be potentially damaged by other methods.

Smoke

If you've been in the metaphysical space long, you'll probably know about the cleansing properties of smoke through smudging. Incense, such as sage, is often used to cleanse spaces such as the home or office and this same logic can be applied to crystals as well. Simply light your incense and allow the crystals to slowly pass through the smoke, make sure you're focusing on your intentions of cleansing as the crystals are enveloped in the cleansing smoke. This method can be used with any stone.

Saltwater

The properties of saltwater have been known for thousands of years to be a force of purification and is often used in cleansing ritual tools, it should be no surprise that salt water can be an extremely effective method of crystal purification. To cleanse your stones with saltwater place them in a jar and fill the jar with water and add a pinch of sea salt, actual sea/ocean water can also be used. This method can be very damaging to porous stones and stones that contain metals. Soft Stones (stones with a 5 or lower on the hardness scale) that should never be exposed to salt water include the following: turquoise, lapis lazuli, pearl, coral, amber, and any stone ending in an -ite such as celestite or moldavite. Stones that contain metals like iron ore should also never be cleansed with salt water such as: pyrite, hematite, red jasper, and hematoid quartz.

Rice

It might be surprising to find out that crystals can be cleansed with rice. Rice has extremely absorbent properties that extend to much more than just moisture. It can take in any energies that are stored in a crystal similar to the way that rice can pull out moisture from electronic devices. Simply bury your stone in a jar of rice and leave for 24 hours. This method is safe to use with any type of stone.

Sound

Sound can be a useful method of cleansing, especially if you're attempting to cleanse a large quantity of crystals. This is done by placing the crystals in front of you or on an altar and using any sound creating device such as singing bowls or bells. If you're more musically inclined you can even use your favorite instrument or develop your own cleansing chant. Ring your bells or sing your chants for approximately 5 minutes or so while focusing your intention on cleansing your crystals, this method is safe to use with any type of stone.

Meditation/Breath

You can cleanse your stones while meditating with the added benefit of cleansing your own aura in the process. Find a peaceful place to meditate and clearly state and focus upon your intentions of cleansing. Feel the cleansing forces go through your body and emanating outwards with every exhale, enveloping your crystals. Do this for approximately 10 minutes or until you feel that the energies from your crystals have been neutralized.

Charging

Crystals do not have an infinite amount of energy and from the moment they're pulled from the earth they start radiating that energy in increasingly diminishing amounts. This can be remedied through the charging of your crystals. Crystals are charged in much the same way that they're cleansed, the main difference in the methods is the intention that you set when conduct the ritual. You should take the same precautions to protect your crystals as you do when cleansing, such as making sure you aren't exposing soft stones or stones that have metals in them to moisture.

Sun and moonlight are two of the most common ways you can charge your stones, it's probably the most popular method due to the fact that you can cleanse them and charge them at the same time. Simply place them on a window seal as you would when cleansing and allow the energies from the heavens to do their work. If your stone isn't damaged by water submerging them in moon water is a great way to charge your stones, moon water is created by leaving a jar of water on a window seal at night for a few hours, the energetic light from the moon charges the water which can then be used in variety of way, in this case charging your crystals.

You can also charge your crystals through meditation, similar to the way that you can cleanse the crystals through this method. The main difference is when charging with meditation you need to ensure that you clearly state your intention to charge, focus on channeling the earth energies through your body and into the crystals, rejuvenating their power. As stated before this method is extremely useful when charging a large quantity of crystals at a time. Your crystals can also be charged with the smoke method, just like with meditation the primary difference in cleansing and charging with smoke is ensuring proper intention and focusing on the task of charging.

www.ingramcontent.com/pod-product-compliance
Lightning Source LLC
Chambersburg PA
CBHW061324120726

48001CB00002B/671